THE TIN TAᴸᴸᴿᴺACLE

Memories of Craigantlet Mission Hall
1912-2001

by Jean Shields

Then they that feared the Lord spake often one to another,
and the Lord hearkened and heard it and a book of
remembrance was written before Him for them that feared the
Lord, and that thought upon His Name.

*"And they shall be mine said the Lord of hosts in that day when
I make up my jewels."*
Malachi 3v16-17

ISBN 978-0-9564515-2-1
© Copyright Jean Shields June 2010

Published and Printed by Award Publishing
email: cedricwilson@live.co.uk

Contents

Preamble

This is not a scholarly work, for I am no historian and so I am indebted to Mr. Alexander Hanna, who was an avid researcher, for the factual details of this little narrative. My contribution is purely anecdotal and dependent on a rather fitful memory. But the characters I portray were well known to me and my recollections of them are warm and precious. They were my family and my folk and the influence they had on my life is profound. There have been many others associated with the Mission Hall over the years but they are outside my remit and I only mention some of them in passing. As the apostle Paul states, "We speak that we do know, and testify that we have seen." I am aware of my limitations and so apologise to anyone who feels there are too many omissions. Their names are recorded in the annals of eternity and in the hearts of those who knew them best.

Founding Fathers

The townland of Craigantlet is a small area adjacent to Newtownards, Dundonald and Holywood. For most of the local churches it is an outpost of their empire and as there was no public building there before 1912, it tended to be bypassed by them, although it is on record that some open air services were held there at the beginning of the twentieth century under the auspices of Dundonald Presbyterian Church. A rural community, it consisted mainly of small farmers and workers in a quarry owned by Samuel Boyd of Ballymiscaw. As the result of a mission held by Faith Mission Pilgrims in Bethesda Mission Hall, Dundonald in 1908, a number of local people came to faith in Jesus Christ and were keen to bring the Gospel message to neighbouring areas. Among these were two brothers, Hugh and William McMillan, and it was they who obtained the site for a tent mission in Craigantlet which was instrumental in the building of the Hall. Symbolically it was at a crossroads, a place where one may change direction, adjacent to the local shop and a public house, in a field noted for cock fighting and other dubious activities. It was here that two Scottish Pilgrims, Mr. Guild from Dundee and Mr. McDonald from the Island of Tiree, pitched their tent on the 10th June 1911 and prepared to do battle against the forces of evil. It seemed as if they had landed in the lions' den, for the locals were hostile and threatened to cut the guy ropes, allowing the tent to collapse. However, early antagonism seems have abated or turned to apathy, and the mission proceeded. Results however, were disappointing, for although a number of people attended, there were no outward signs of a movement of the Holy Spirit and after five weeks the Pilgrims were of a mind to pick up the pegs and move on. Before the final decision they visited the home of Mr. David Orr, a godly man and an elder in 1st Holywood Presbyterian Church. His grandson, Derek Orr, still lives on the family farm at Killarn. His daughter Mary became the wife of Mr. James Colville, who led the Prayer Union in Tullynagardy for many years. Their daughter Margaret is still an active member of Craigantlet Prayer Union. Another daughter Sarah married Mr. James McKee who, with his family, subsequently ran Ballybeen Mission Hall in Dundonald.

On Mr. Orr's advice the Pilgrims took courage and continued on for another eight weeks, the mission concluding on the 10th September 1911. By that time the meetings were crowded and some sixty souls came to faith, most of whom were local farmers. The whole character of the countryside was changed and became a sober, hardworking community of worshipping people.

During the mission the Pilgrims stayed at the home of Mr. and Mrs. James Lindsay of Dunlady and their teenage daughter Jean, who became a convert. After her marriage to Mr. John Musgrave she continued to live there and bring up their six children. They were a musical family and in turn played the organ in the Mission Hall until the seventies. Their son James still lives in the family home and it was there that the Craigantlet Prayer Union was founded after the mission, and continued to meet under Mr. Lindsay's leadership until the Hall was built. He was a man of considerable presence and we called him the Bishop of Craigantlet.

It must be said that the building of the Hall was the result of much hard work and self-denial on the part of the local Christians and it is significant that it was opened the following year, 1912, furnished and fit for the Master's use. There were few planning restrictions in those days but the founding fathers were wise and ensured that the building and site would permanently be a centre for evangelical worship.

The Tin Tabernacle

High on the hilltop it stood for nearly ninety years braving the elements, a little corrugated iron structure, surrounded by sedimentary rocks, as rugged and hardy as the people who built it and made it their place of worship. Lashed by rain and shaken by storm it remained firm, a landmark and a witness to all who passed by. The inside was as simple as its exterior.

A tiny square entrance hall, fitted with pegs for hats and coats, opened into the main building, consisting of a central aisle and flanked by two rows of sturdy wooden forms not very conducive to comfort until latter times when they were padded and cushioned in red velvet. A coal stove graced the centre of the aisle with a pipe extending through the roof. I remember it as a sullen fire that often filled the room with a heavy haze of smoke. It was replaced in later years by a potbellied Esse which emitted an intense dry heat. Three paraffin lights hung from the ceiling, one of which was replaced by a Calor gas light that glowed warmly. Faith, Hope and Charity we called them. The advent of electricity to the district in the early fifties simplified all our lives. Hours of trimming, filling and fuelling were replaced by the press of a switch. A text at the front proclaimed 'Jesus Christ is Lord' and beneath it was a sturdy platform with an attached lectern. It was fronted by a red curtain, held in place by brass rings - I have forgotten how many, although as a child I counted them every Sunday. I suppose you could say it was part of my religion. Two large ornately designed pulpit chairs adorned it. To the left stood a Mason and Hamlin organ with twelve stops, which played soft or loud music according to the pedal pressure of the organist's feet. The room was bright, with three large windows at each side. The walls were panelled to keep in the heat and decorated with useful slogans; 'Faith Brings Victory' and 'Prayer Changes Things' - are two I recall.

Within its walls we praised and prayed and were ministered unto and many, both young and old, came to a saving faith kneeling beside its hard wooden seats. To them and others the Tin Tabernacle became the "House of God and the very gate of Heaven".

Early Memories of Craigantlet

My family (The Reas) came from Ballykeel to live at Craigantlet in 1931. My father having purchased the farm on whose ground the Hall was built. Every year he received a nominal rent of ten shillings for the use of the ground and returned it via the collection plate. He had attended the tent mission twenty years earlier but being on the Naval Reserve he was called up in 1914 and served in the Naval Brigade until the Armistice in 1918, most of that time being spent in a German prison camp. My mother had two children before the Great War broke out and two more after the cessation of hostilities. I was the youngest and the only daughter. Both of my parents were converted through the Faith Mission at a mission held in Ballyhill, County Antrim, sometime before their marriage in 1905. The Hall became one of my mother's greatest joys and she attended faithfully. The last meeting at which she was present was on Sunday 16th July 1961 and the following evening she went home to be with her Lord. Two days later her cortege halted briefly outside its gates on route to Clandeboye Cemetery just a few weeks before the Fiftieth Anniversary Services were held on August 26th and 27th. My father is pictured on that day with the last remaining foundation members of the Prayer Union, his face ravaged by grief, but still a strong, courageous follower of the way. He joined my mother in Glory in 1968. The message on their headstone says it all in three words, 'Saved by Grace'.

Within a few years of coming to live at Craigantlet I joined Creighton's Green Sunday School and was enrolled as a pupil in Ballymiscaw P.E.S. We all became regular worshippers at the Mission Hall and my father joined the rota of preachers. Sunday by Sunday we walked abreast up the hill. Often in the clear summer evenings the peal of bells from Holywood Parish Church was wafted on the still air, a gentle soothing sound long faded and superseded by the omnipresent screech of motor cars. From the small car park one could look over the Mission Hall fence to where the rocky outcrop fell away sharply to level undulating pasture sweeping downward to the shores of Belfast Lough, before the Forestry Commission planted the area with trees. As evening shadows gathered, an arc of light spread fan-like across the eastern sky, the first bright beam from the Copeland Island Lighthouse, while short sharp flashes responded from the dark promontory of Blackhead. The light scent of whin blossoms filled the air and the darkening landscape grew luminous as the sinking sun reflected the pale yellow flowers growing from a harsh and prickly plant, one that farmers sought in vain to eradicate. Truly "He has made everything beautiful in His time".

Lord, it is eventide

Lord, it is eventide: the light of day is waning;
Far o'er the golden land earth's voices faint and fall;
Lowly we pray to Thee for strength and love sustaining,
Lowly we ask of Thee Thy peace upon us all.
O grant unto our souls, -

Light that groweth not pale
With day's decrease,
Love that never can fail
Till life shall cease;
Joy no trial can mar,
Hope that shineth afar
Faith serene as a star,
And Christ's own peace.

Lord, it is eventide: we turn to Thee for healing,
Like those of Galilee who came at close of day;
Speak to our waiting souls, their hidden founts unsealing;
Touch us with hands divine that take our sin away.
O grant unto our souls, -

Saviour, Thou knowest all, the trial and temptations,
Knowest the wilfulness and waywardness of youth;
Help us to cling to Thee, our Strength and our Salvation,
Help us to find in Thee the one eternal Truth.
O grant unto our souls, -

Lord, it is eventide: our hearts await Thy giving,
Wait for that peace divine that none can take away,
Peace that shall lift our souls to loftier heights of living,
Till we abide with Thee in everlasting day.
O Grant unto our souls, -

"The Meeting"

As a small child I sat on the hard, high seat swinging my short legs, as all children must do when their feet don't reach the floor, and often irritating the person in front. When we sang the old hymn:

> 'Joyful, joyful will the meeting be,
> When from sin our hearts are pure and free',

I knew that my heart was not pure and free from sin, for I was often fidgety and restless as the meeting progressed, in spite of my mother's reproving looks. I have not yet attained that state of grace although seventy-odd years have elapsed, but I know that that particular joy is reserved for me in the sweet by-and-by.

One thing embarrassed me more than any other - to drop my collection penny and hear it careering up the length of the Hall before collapsing with a loud clank at the very front. There was no way to hide my shame for I had no penny to drop in the plate. Strangely, I quite enjoyed the scenario when it happened to someone else, as it sometimes did. One small incident from those far off days is firmly etched in my memory. It was a warm summer evening and the door had been left open to provide a circulation of air. Half-way through the service there was a diversion. My eyes popped out like organ stops as I watched our black and tan collie dog wander slowly but unerringly up the aisle and lie down quietly at my father's feet. He had been a stray who came to us frightened and starving. My mother had gently nourished him back to health and we all loved him dearly. Perhaps he felt he had something in common with us all – helpless, needy creatures who had found a home and grace abounding.

The service had a simple format, rousing hymns from Songs of Victory, a short season of chain prayer, a Bible reading and a brief homily by a local speaker. No ladies spoke from the platform although some took part in prayer. This was something of an anomaly for many perhaps, as most of the Pilgrims were and are ladies and their preaching is just as effective as that of their male counterparts. After the meeting my mother and I sometimes walked a little way with some solitary lady, and so friendships were consolidated and the Sabbath ended with a quiet gentle unwinding.

Personalities

What a well- dressed group of respectable people they were,
the Mission Hall folk! Ladies in long, dark coats with
matching hats; men, close shaven and correct, in navy or
grey suits and stiff white collars. Even for children, casual
wear did not exist, only Sunday clothes and working clothes.
The lady seated at the very front was Mrs. Boyd, the organist,
who lived in the Quarry House opposite the Hall. It too has
been demolished and is being replaced even as I write.
Behind Mrs. Boyd sat her mother, Mrs. Shanks, a very
missionary minded lady who introduced us to O.M.S., a
Mission still close to the heart of the Prayer Union. My
mother and I sat behind Mrs. Maxwell who sang beautifully
from the Tonic Solfa and wore a huge hat pin that seemed
to go right through her head. In the corner seat was Hugh
Hogg, who attended the meetings until he was over ninety,
walking all the way from McNeill's Farm, about one and a
half miles away. Beside him sat Mr. Joe Hollinger, the Prayer
Union representative who succeeded James Lindsay. He was
a godly man and devoted to the Faith Mission. Behind us
sat a group of young people, some of them lads who had
wandered up from the Crossroads where they congregated
in the evenings to chat and smoke or play quoits with horse
shoes in the adjacent field, but never on a Sunday to the best
of my knowledge. Initially they exchanged whispers but

soon settled down as the service progressed. Respectful silence was the norm at the meeting. On the right hand side sat Mr. Sam McWilliams, a widower, who lived in Craigantlet House on the Dunlady Road. He was deputed to make the announcements and did so in a clear, cultured voice. Behind him sat his brother-in-law, Richard Boal, who owned a small farm on Whinney Hill. My brother, who in later years preached on the rota, married his daughter and they lived there until 1973, when it was sold and became the popular Riding School 'Birr House'. Mrs. Boal was a very efficient lady and took an active part in catering for the annual Conference. Beside them sat James Lowry, a devout Christian and faithful servant. A story is told of him that he was given some apples by a young man who later told him they'd been stolen from a neighbour's orchard. This troubled his conscience so much that he apologised to the owner and offered to pay for them. My father sat beside a namesake, though not a relation, Mr. John Rea, who was the Superintendent in Creighton's Green Sunday School. He and his wife were fine singers and a great asset to the praise. By their sides sat Mr. Sam Graham, who cycled all the way from the Bangor Road. He had a family of seven, and years later they occupied a full seat in the Mission Hall. His daughters Isa, Ciss, Jean and Nan all attended the Prayer Union till the end of their lives. The youngest, Nan (Magowan) was the last to go home to Glory in 2008. William Pettigrew occupied the next seat. Upon Mr. Rea's death in 1947, he became Sunday School Superintendent at Creighton's Green. He died in 1960 and is buried in the plot next to my parents in Clandeboye - friend and neighbour still. His daughter Grace has devoted her life to missionary service with O.M.F in the Far East, particularly in Thailand and Singapore. After William's death his brother Harry took over the family farm and attended the Hall for many years.

Further back sat Mr. and Mrs. Musgrave with their family of six children. The eldest, Jean, succeeded Mrs. Boyd at the organ and her sister Margaret took over that office when Jean married and presided for over thirty years. Some of the foundation members, including Mr. Lindsay, had now retired but still took their turn on the preaching rota. Another of these was Mr. Sam McKee whose son David with his wife Agnes were stalwarts at the Hall for many years, taking part in all the activities both practically and devotionally. Their son David is the present Prayer Union representative and their daughter Margaret, who with her husband Tom Scott, spent many years in Brazil with O.M.S, share that responsibility.

Most of these men were "sons of the sod" and their spiritual roots too were deeply embedded and fruitful. They served the Lord in their daily tasks and were known for their integrity in the market place, the sale yard and the auction rooms. Theirs was a holistic faith that covered every aspect of their lives at home with their families, and in the wider world of commerce.

Happy Are They

Happy are they, they that love God,
Whose hearts have Christ confest,
Who by His Cross have found their life,
And 'neath His yoke their rest

Glad is the praise, sweet are the songs,
When they together sing
And strong the prayers that bow the ear
Of heaven's eternal King.

Christ to their homes giveth His peace,
And makes their love His own;
But ah, what tares the evil one
Hath in His garden sown!

Sad were our lot, evil this earth,
Did not its sorrows prove
The path whereby the sheep may find
The fold of Jesus' love.

Then shall they know, they that love Him,
How all their pain is good;
And death itself cannot unbind
Their happy brotherhood.

Yattendon Hymnal, No. 34, 1899;
based on Charles Coffin, 1676-1749

"Lighten Our Darkness"

Our peaceful and pastoral setting with its measured seasons was about to change. Once again the dogs of war threatened, and in 1939 the whole of Europe erupted into World War Two. Life became dangerous and moved at a fast pace as the great war-machine advanced. Farmers' lives changed completely, ruled by milk quotas, compulsory ploughing and a bureaucracy previously unknown, in the great struggle to feed to nation. Yet our little prayer group met regularly for prayer each week, resting their weary limbs in the quiet of the sanctuary to pour out their souls to God for their families, the district and nation now under threat. Around this time in 1939 a mission was scheduled and was conducted by two Faith Mission Pilgrims, William Black from Belfast, who later became Irish Director for the Faith Mission, and Mark Stone from southern Ireland who emigrated to Canada after the War. This proved an eventful time, for fear gripped many people. Destruction by bombing lay ahead together with the threat of invasion, so they sought refuge in a renewed faith. Out of the blackout that shrouded the countryside in an eerie darkness they came into the warmth and comfort of the Tin Tabernacle. There is something reassuring about the smell of burning lamp oil, I think. Perhaps it reminds us of the little night light that glowed for us in the dark when as children we woke in the night from a disturbing dream. Mr. Black played his accordion and we sang the familiar hymns, learnt new choruses and went home with lighter footsteps and uplifted spirits. Once again we had the opportunity "to grasp with a firmer hand the eternal grace" and a good number of local people availed themselves of it. In particular I would mention a small Scotsman, Sammy Montgomery who worked in the quarry. Sammy had "tried the broken cisterns" and his eagerness to share the New Life he had received in Christ was wonderful to see. He came with his family to live within a few yards of the Mission Hall and both he and his wife and sister-in-law dedicated themselves to the service of the Lord. Sammy stood in the cold porch welcoming worshippers and giving out hymn books while Mary kept the Hall in spotless order, and both prayed faithfully and fervently for friends and family. It was after this mission that Mr. Alexander Hanna took responsibility for the services, a position he was to hold for over forty years. Outside speakers were invited to conduct the services and more young people began to attend, especially after the blitzes of 1941, when the countryside was flooded with evacuees from Belfast. Some of the foundation members were beginning to feel the "burden and heat of the day" and were ready for innovation. Their joy remained undimmed and they were happy to take a back seat whilst still lending their experience to the new leadership. Hard work and wartime conditions took their toll and slowly, over the years, they went "marching upward to Zion, the beautiful City of God". I believe that the last survivor of the 1911 Mission was Mrs. Sarah McKee, a daughter of Mr. Orr whose counsel encouraged the Pilgrims to go the second mile and conduct a marathon mission lasting thirteen weeks. She died in 1989. Her son Ivan represented O.M.S in England for a number of years and her grandson James is on the team of WEC. The blessing of 1911 has filtered through to the present time and a growing number of young people, whose grandparents and great grandparents shared in those glory days, are now in active Christian service and fill the pews of many of our local churches.

Profile of Mr. Alexander Hanna

As the longest serving leader of the fellowship in Craigantlet, Mr. Alexander Hanna merits this special mention for his work in the service. Even after his retirement he remained a faithful attender on Sunday evenings and so was associated with the Mission Hall for more than half the period of its existence. Sandy, as we affectionately called him, lived in the townland of Ballymiscaw about two miles from the site of Craigantlet Mission Hall. He was the eldest of three children who lost both parents while still in their teens and grew up to be a very godly family devoted to Christian service. Ballymiscaw had been a centre for Christianity since 1854 when Ballymiscaw National School was opened. A Sunday School began there immediately and five years later the district felt the effects of the '59 revival, when the little School House was crowded to capacity with seeking souls. Of the many converts, Mr. Sam Boyd was the one who later organised regular meetings in the School House under the auspices of Dundonald Presbyterian Church. His grandson, Mr. Jim Boyd, succeeded him in 1930 and being a young man he was specifically interested in the youth of the district. Ably assisted by his two sisters, Beth and Janey, he superintended the Sunday School, captained a Boys Brigade Company, led a Christian Endeavour, set up a Girls Brigade Company under Janey's captaincy and managed a football team and other youth activities. In 1931 the Boyd Memorial Hall was built in memory of his grandfather, and Jim continued to pioneer the work from there until his death in 1980. Many young people were influenced by Jim Boyd, including the Hanna family and a group of fine young adults were connected with the various activities in the Boyd Memorial Hall and it was from that background that Sandy responded to the call to lead the work in Craigantlet. The Boyd Memorial Hall still stands although it is no longer in use.

Sandy was in his early twenties when he became responsible for the Mission Hall Fellowship in 1940. Under his leadership many outstanding evangelists of the time graced the platform of the Tin Tabernacle. The local government kindly granted a ration of two gallons of petrol per month to convey speakers from the nearest point of public transport, and Mr. David McKee Senior carried out the duty of transport during the war, and indeed for many more years. Under Sandy's leadership the Mission Hall was extended and a new brick frontage was erected; the car park was extended making the plain little building look quite impressive.

Mr. Hanna's personal life was a triumph of grace over adversity. In 1947 he married Miss Mirlie Caldwell, a talented young woman from Dundonald. Under her direction, a Ladies' Choir was formed and her devotion to her Lord and the witness of the Mission Hall attracted many more young people. Sadly Mirlie went home to be with the Lord in 1954, leaving a family of three little girls, the youngest only days old. For one who had lost his own parents while still young the following years were bleak indeed, but Sandy rallied and courageously recommitted himself to the task and so the work continued under his leadership until his retirement in 1984. He joined his much loved Mirlie in the Heavenly home in 1998. Dundonald Presbyterian Church, where he was an Elder, was packed to capacity for his funeral and he was interred in the family plot in Saint Elizabeth's Churchyard nearby. His legacy to the Mission Hall was immeasurable. He recorded its archives in great detail in 1985, publishing a book entitled These Three Hundred and Forty Years which is a history of Dundonald Presbyterian Church and other Christian fellowships in the area including Craigantlet. It is from this work that the historical background of this present account is taken. He was an avid researcher, a keen student and precise recorder, but above all a sincere follower of Jesus Christ and a witness to the power of the Holy Spirit in his life, "His works do follow him".

Red Dahlias And Tomato Sandwiches

The most important day in the Mission Hall calendar was one Saturday each August when the annual Conference and Rejoining was held. It was presided over by the Irish Director of the Faith Mission who in my earliest days was Mr. J B. McLean, a Scotsman, as many of the Faith Mission leaders were. I never knew what the initials J.B. stood for. We tended to address people as Mr., Mrs. or Miss and it wasn't unusual to be acquainted with a person for a long period of time without knowing their Christian name, until it was revealed in their obituary in the Belfast Telegraph. Accompanying J.B. was a selection of the best Faith Mission speakers, Pilgrims and singers guaranteed to rouse the most faint-hearted Prayer Union member in Craigantlet. What a frenzy of preparation took place! The ladies set off immediately after dinner (what we now call lunch) with their covered baskets containing dusters and tea cloths, home-churned butter and sandwich fillings. Eight white loaves had to be cut, buttered and filled, usually with thinly sliced tomatoes or corned beef from a little tin with a key attached for not so easy opening. But first of all the big tea chest was hauled out and the cups were unwrapped from their newspaper covering. They were thoroughly washed and dried at Mrs. Boal's insistence, although they always seemed perfectly clean to me. The shutter from the top window was placed across the backs of two forms and everyone worked with a will, happily slicing, buttering and filling. A spotless white sheet was draped over the impromptu table and the food temptingly arranged on it. The seats were all thoroughly dusted, floors swept and everything made spic and span. The crowning glory was a vase of dark red dahlias adorning the front of the platform.

The first meeting commenced at 3 o'clock and continued until five o'clock. People began to arrive half an hour early to get a good seat or indeed any seat, for it was always a full house. The singing was hearty, the sermons long and quite beyond my comprehension, but I enjoyed hearing the Pilgrims' accounts of missions and their personal testimonies. By five o'clock we were more than ready to "partake of the good things provided". How tasty those sandwiches were! And the slices of fruit loaf (sometimes called 'Believers bread' because of its association with Christian gatherings) rich, dark and spicy, were like manna from heaven, washed down with strong dark tea well sweetened, for few people drank tea without sugar before the war. Visitors sometimes "stretched their legs" down the hill in preparation for the second session while the workers "gathered up the fragments". It didn't require twelve baskets to contain them! Some went home at this stage in time for the evening milking but others arrived cycling from Newtownards or Dundonald, hanging their caps in the porch and pocketing their bicycle clips before taking their seats for the evening meeting at 6 o'clock. After a further two hours the final 'Amen' was pronounced and the last 'Hallelujah' shouted and we sang with renewed vigour "Bringing in the Sheaves". Sabbath day's rest ensued and we all foregathered on Monday evening to wash the big white cups, dry and wrap them carefully in their paper packaging and put them neatly away for another year. The Conference meetings were reviewed in detail, we drank a final cup of tea together and sang 'How Good is the God we Adore', Mr. McWilliams blessed us all in his kindly way and committed us afresh to God's care and service. It was a weekend of blessing, reunion and joy. The ladies who officiated at the conference were Mrs. Lindsay and her daughter Mrs. Musgrave, two very gracious ladies, Mrs. Boal, highly efficient and diligent, and Mrs. Wilson, a lovely woman who wore a shiny necklace and carried a bag of sweets in her pocket which she shared with a quiet little girl who, from her mother's side, observed and memorised all that took place. My mother and these other ladies all played their part in preparing and serving, sharing Martha's gift making a meal fit for the Master himself. In later years the Conference was held in February. It was a "shortened version" being at seven-thirty with tea at the end. Preparations were made at home and laid out just before the service. Gone were the days of five hour Conferences and thirteen week missions. The world had moved on, and February produced no red dahlias, but the sandwich fillings were more varied and there was a wider choice of homemade delicacies. The team of workers was led by Miss Edith Milligan and later by her niece Mrs. Hazel McKee. I still find it hard to believe that so many people were catered for in a small Hall with so few facilities.

Conference Antiphon

'We're feasting on the living bread,
We're drinking at the fountain head
And who so drinketh Jesus said
Shall never, never thirst again.
Men - What, never thirst again?
Women - No, never thirst again? (repeat)
All - And who so drinketh Jesus said
Shall never, never thirst again.'

All Good Gifts Around Us

Next in importance to the Conferences were the Harvest Services held over a weekend in October. Such meetings were popular in the churches but it was not until Sandy took charge that they were held in the Mission Hall. The whole countryside attended for we all lived close to the land and shared in the sowing and reaping processes. Indeed our livelihood depended on it, for a good season meant a secure winter for folk and flock alike. As children we watched the ploughing, planting and growth on our way to and from school. On a short, cold winter day a farmer with his team of horses could plough about half an acre, so we were accustomed to seeing neighbours out in the same field from dawn to dusk day after day. We watched the first green shoots appear and rejoiced to see the corn 'abraird' in the early spring sunshine. All through the summer it grew, its lush green turning to gold over the summer holidays. The most common grain crop grown locally is now barley, but in my early years it was oats, or corn as we called it, I always preferred its shining golden straw and delicately drooping ears to the duller more mundane crops of barley or wheat. I am old enough to remember it being reaped by a horse drawn mowing machine and hand tied in sheaves before being stacked in groups of four to form a 'stook'. What a great invention the Massey Harris binder was, depositing the sheaves neatly tied with binder twine. That was the forerunner of the great combine harvester which clears the fields as if by magic.

By mid-October we were normally ready to celebrate God's rich bounty and to give thanks for dry weather and the gift of health to garner His generous provision. The Hall was lavishly decorated with the fruits of our labour. Outsized vegetables adorned every available inch of space and the air was redolent with the scent of large yellow and white chrysanthemums. The platform was always flanked on either side with golden sheaves spread widely at the base. One small incident comes to mind as I recall those happy occasions. We were about to sing that most popular of all Harvest hymns 'Come ye Thankful People, Come'. I glanced down to position my right foot on the organ pedal ready for the opening chord and looked into the terrified eyes of a little field mouse emerging from the sheaf of oats only inches away. I hoped frantically that he wouldn't disappear under the pedal to be stamped to death by my large pounding feet, but he retreated, just in time, back to the safety of his little straw house. I like to think he lived to tell the tale for he was a shrewd little shrew with no intention of becoming a church mouse. The services continued on Monday evenings and some of the best speakers of the times addressed us, including the late Dr Roy Magee who is remembered for his work as a peace negotiator during and after the troubles. Also Dr W Magee Craig a former moderator of the General Assembly. A favourite subject was that of the rich farmer who pulled down his barns and built greater. I don't think any of our families were in his category, but we had enough and to spare and the old Harvest Hymn rang out loud and clear, 'All Good Gifts Around Us are sent from Heaven above, Then thank the Lord, O Thank the Lord for all His Love'. Praise was a very important part of our worship and the singing was always hearty with some feet tapping and waving of hymn books. Hymns reflected the evangelical message of the Faith Mission and the doctrine of holy living which it promoted. Depicted on the cover of the old Songs of Victory hymn book was a soldier in full military uniform and equipped with a sword and shield. It contained about four hundred hymns, many of which I knew by heart for my mother often sang them as she washed, swept, baked or ironed. I suppose many of them would be considered politically incorrect nowadays with their frequent references to "the heathen" and "men benighted". Still many sad souls were rescued from despair by their simple message of salvation by faith alone, in Christ alone, and there was no feminist movement to object to such lines as 'Jesus died for all mankind'. In later years we sang from the old Redemption Hymnbook with its choice of over a thousand hymns. One of the most popular and well loved was 'I have a Shepherd'. It was said to be a favourite of Joey Dunlop of motorcycling fame and was sung at his funeral. It is interesting to speculate that Joey, who consistently led the way in his field of sport, should in his private life be a follower of the Good Shepherd and enjoy a spiritual relationship with Christ. One hymn that my children, Paul and Mark (who like myself attended the Mission Hall from an early age) particularly liked was 'Marching on in the Light of God' with its rousing chorus 'A robe of White, a Crown of Gold', indeed they had their own special version of it which began 'A Robot White'. Within recent years the Faith Mission has produced a fine new hymn book containing modern hymns and choruses while still retaining most of the old favourites.

Let us sing of His love

Let us sing of His love once again,
of the love that can never decay,
of the blood of the Lamb Who was slain,
till we praise Him again in that day

I believe Jesus saves!
and His blood makes me whiter than snow!
I believe Jesus saves!
and His blood makes me whiter than snow!

There is cleansing and healing for all
who will wash in the life-giving flood;
there is perfect deliverance and joy
to be had in this world through the blood

Even now, while we taste of His love,
we are filled with delight through His name;
but what will it be when above,
we shall join in the song of the Lamb?

Then we'll march in His Name till we come,
at His bidding to cease from the fight,
and our Saviour shall welcome us home
to the regions of glory and light.

So with banner unfurled to the breeze
our motto shall "Holiness" be,
till the crown from His hand we receive,
and the King in His glory we see.

I am sure we shall win,
for we fight in the strength of our King.
I am sure we shall win,
for we fight in the strength of our King.

F Bottome (1833-94)

Come, ye that love the Lord

Come, ye that love the Lord
and let your joys be known;
join in a song with sweet accord,
join in a song with sweet accord
and thus surround the throne,
and thus surround the throne.

We're marching to Zion!
Beautiful, beautiful Zion!
We're marching upward to Zion,
the beautiful city of God!

Let those refuse to sing
who never knew our God
but children of the heavenly King,
but children of the heavenly king
must speak their joys abroad,
must speak their joys abroad.

The hill of Zion yields
a thousand sacred sweets,
before we reach the heavenly fields,
before we reach the heavenly fields
or walk the golden streets,
or walk the golden streets.

Then let our songs abound
and every tear be dry:
we're marching through Immanuel's ground,
we're marching through Immanuel's ground,
to fairer worlds on high,
to fairer worlds on high.

Isaac Watts (1674-1748)

Marching on in the light of God

Marching on in the light of God,
marching on, I'm marching on;
up the path that the Master trod,
marching, marching on.

A robe of white, a crown of gold,
a harp, a home, a mansion fair,
a victor's palm, a joy untold,
are mine when I get there.
For Jesus is my Saviour, He washed my sins away,
paid my debt on Calvary's mountain;
I'm happy in His dying love, singing all the day,
I'm living, yes, I'm living in the fountain.

Marching on through the hosts of sin,
victory's mine while I've Christ within.

Marching on while the worldlings sneer,
perfect love casteth out all fear.

Marching on in the Spirit's might,
more than conqueror in every fight.

Marching on to the realms above,
there to sing of redeeming love.

R Johnson
Copyright Control

There's a Saviour from all sin

There's a Saviour from all sin;
if you only let Him in
to your heart, He there will reign,
while you trust Him.
He will put the evil out,
save from every fear and doubt,
and you'll soon begin to shout,
"Hallelujah!"

Hallelujah! Hallelujah!
Jesus is my Saviour King,
He doth full salvation bring,
Hallelujah! Hallelujah!
Now with heart and voice I sing
Hallelujah!

Jesus is a wondrous Name,
now and evermore the same
He can cleanse from every stain,
only trust Him.
He will fill your soul with joy,
and your talents will employ,
Satan's kingdom to destroy,
Hallelujah!

If from every sin you part,
and let Christ have all your heart,
you need fear no fiery dart,
while you trust Him.
For while Jesus reigns within,
you are proof against all sin,
and His perfect peace you win,
Hallelujah!

John George Govan (1861-1927)

Full salvation! Full salvation!

Full Salvation! Full Salvation!
lo! the fountain opened wide
streams through every land and nation
from the Saviour's wounded side.
Full Salvation! Full Salvation!
Full Salvation! Full Salvation!
streams an endless crimson tide.

Oh, the glorious revelation!
see the cleansing current flow,
washing stains of condemnation
whiter than the driven snow!
Full Salvation!
oh! the rapturous bliss to know!

Love's resistless current sweeping
all the regions deep within;
thought and wish and senses keeping
now, and every instant, clean.
Full Salvation!
from the guilt and power of sin.

Life immortal, heaven descending,
lo! my heart the Spirit's shrine!
God and man in oneness blending,
oh, what fellowship is mine!
Full Salvation!
raised in Christ to life divine!

Care and doubting, gloomy sorrow,
fear and grief are mine no more;
faith knows naught of dark tomorrow
for my Saviour goes before.
Full Salvation!
full and free for evermore.

F Bottome (1823-94)

Under the burdens of guilt and care

Under the burdens of guilt and care,
many a spirit is grieving,
who in the joy of the Lord might share,
life everlasting receiving.

Life! life! eternal life!
Jesus alone is the Giver!
Life! life! abundant life!
Glory to Jesus for ever!

Burdened one, why will you longer bear
sorrows from which He releases?
Open your heart, and, rejoicing, share
life more abundant in Jesus!

Leaving the mountain, the streamlet grows,
flooding the vale with a river;
so from the hill of the Cross, there flows
life more abundant for ever.

Oh, for the floods on the thirsty land!
Oh, for a mighty revival!
Oh, for a sanctified fearless band,
ready to hail its arrival!

W Leslie © Unidentified

Annversaries

Four special Anniversary Services were held during the lifetime of the Mission Hall. The first and by far the largest was held in 1936, twenty-five years after the eventful tent mission. In the intervening years, Pilgrim McDonald had returned to his farming background on the Island of Tiree, while Mr. Guild had become a Minister in the Church of Scotland, but they both returned to share in the Jubilee Conference. A photograph taken at that event shows a total of a hundred and fifty-one people, I'm told. It is difficult to imagine how they were accommodated in the original little building, but no doubt the ladies rose to the occasion and everyone was well fed both physically and spiritually. It is reckoned that twenty-seven converts of the original mission were present and it was long remembered as a time of great rejoicing. Twenty-five years later in 1961 a Golden Jubilee service was conducted by Reverend Duncan Campbell, whose name is associated with the Revival movement on the Isle of Lewis in 1947. A photograph shows six stalwarts of the first mission still actively involved in the fellowship. The Diamond Jubilee was celebrated in 1971. The main speaker on that occasion was Reverend J. Finlay from Castledawson. Tea was provided in the usual lavish fashion and a celebratory cake cut by Mrs. Musgrave, daughter of the first Prayer Union representative and a convert of the 1911 mission. The seventy-fifth anniversary was celebrated in 1986 under the chairmanship of Mr. David McGilton, when Mr. Hanna gave a talk on the early history of the work. By that time there were few foundation members left here on earth to recall the joyful events of 1911, but their names and personalities were remembered with love and pride. The gathering was addressed by Dr. Grace Pettigrew whose family had a long and close relationship with the Mission Hall. Dr. Pettigrew was at home on deputation from Manorem Hospital in Thailand where she served as a medical missionary. She based her message on the verse 'Apart from Me there is no God' giving us insights into her contacts with Hindu people. It was a time of nostalgia, of joy and tears, for even we second generation members were growing old. Change was on the way, evening shadows were beginning to darken our skies and this proved to be the last anniversary service to be held in the Mission Hall. Life had moved on, we were living in the cult of the young. Most families owned a car and could travel farther afield to where more youth facilities were offered. The era of the Mission Hall was drawing to a close. Free churches and house groups sprang up around us offering more attractions, singing groups were forming with guitar accompaniment, new hymns and choruses proliferated and worship was transformed. While in general approving of this change of emphasis we 'golden oldies' continued in our traditional way for a little longer, but our God Who is from Everlasting to Everlasting is also a Great Innovator, Who has declared 'I will do a new thing'. So it was time to widen our horizons. After all, most of us lived in modern houses and farming methods had changed out of all recognition, so why should the Church of Jesus Christ remain in the past, glorious as that had been? A slogan used by Youth for Christ was 'anchored to the Rock, geared to the times' and gradually the message was taken on board and change was accepted. Life in the Spirit should always be an adventure. We learn from the past, live in the present and look forward to the future. 'He that sat in the midst of the throne said "Behold I make all things new"'.

25ᵗʰ Anniversary
A few of those who were saved and blessed during the Craigantlet Mission in 1911

Foundation Members at 50th Anniversary 1961
L–R Joe Hollinger, Mrs James Colville, Mrs Samuel Boyd, Mrs John Musgrave,
Mr Samuel Graham, Mr James Colville, Mr Thomas Rea

60th Anniversary 1971

L-R Unidentified Faith Mission Pilgrim, Mrs William Black, Mr Ellis Govan,
Mr Edward Fox (Irish Director), Mrs Jean Musgrave (Foundation Member),
Mr Sandy Hanna (Prayer Union Representative)

The Prayer Union

From its inception the Prayer Union has been an essential part of the Faith Mission ethos. After a Mission took place, a small group would band together, pledged to meet regularly to pray for the work of the Mission, their own locality and Christian witness generally. This practice continues. A representative is appointed, who frequently receives a bulletin from the local Faith Mission office giving details of all the Mission's activities. This news is duly shared with all the members to direct their thoughts and prayers. From time to time a member of the Faith Mission staff visits each Prayer Union to give an update, and a monthly publication is also available, it was originally called 'Bright Words' and contained sermons and articles of encouragement from the Pilgrims, as well as details of missions and Pilgrim's locations. It later appeared under the title 'Life Indeed' and still exists in another format with the title 'First'. Bright Words was to be found in most Faith Mission homes and along with the Christian Herald and Life of Faith, was considered basic Christian reading.

One of the functions of the Prayer Union was to arrange for missions to be held from time to time and these were looked upon as special occasions for prayer and outreach and supported by Prayer Union members from the area which, in my time, meant within cycling or walking distance. It was customary for two Pilgrims to share the work of mission and they usually stayed in the home of a Prayer Union member, visiting in the homes by day and preaching each night, either in a local building or portable hall, or a tent in summer. Some of the missioners I recall were Mr. Edward Fox, who became Irish Director of the Mission, and his co-worker Mr. Jim Johnston who was later ordained as a minister in the Church of Scotland; Mr. Jim Graham who devoted his life to mission work in Swaziland; and Miss Burns who married Mr. William Black, another Irish Director and is still a member of the Former Pilgrims association. More recently was Grace Porter, now Mrs. Howson, wife of the superintendent for central England, and her colleague Miss Esther Hewitt. There were also Gospel campaigns conducted by the Christian Workers Union members, particularly Mr. and Mrs. Wheeler and Messrs Boland and Grant. The last mission held in Craigantlet Mission Hall was led in 1995 by Mr. and Mrs. Roy Dreaning.

Before Mr. Hanna's retirement in 1984, the Prayer Union representative was held jointly by Mr. David McKee, who still retains this position and Mr. Willie Anderson who, with his wife May and son Willie John, still live at the family farm on Whinney Hill. Willie is a true son of the land and has a wide knowledge of husbandry and all things rural. As our Prayer Union representative, he kept a low profile preferring to listen than talk, but his contribution to the subject under study was always measured and wise. I remember a certain evening in the seventies when Ulster was suffering most grievously during the Troubles, we were leaving the meeting after our time of prayer and Bible study and I scrambled into Willie's Land Rover for a lift to my home nearby. An army helicopter buzzed overhead like an outsized bumblebee and as we drove through the gate it swooped low and followed us only feet above our heads until we halted outside my house. We got out and were standing at the back door of the Land Rover while the chopper hovered ever lower and a bright, blinding spotlight focused directly on us. Willie was totally unfazed by all this but I was more than a little nervous. Our military observers saw a man hand two bulky objects to his female passenger and then drive off into the night. As suddenly as it had appeared the search light went out, the helicopter swung round, gained ground and was soon out of sight. After all, what could be more innocent than a farmer driving quietly along a country road and a middle-aged woman trudging up to her front door carrying a turnip and a cabbage? Nobody grows vegetables better than Willie, or shares them more generously, and no-one enjoys them as much as I.

Ladies

While the leadership of the work was always in the hands of men, the devotional life of the Prayer Union could not have carried on without the support of godly women. In particular I recall some who gave many years of service and others who led children's activities.

Mrs. Agnes McCracken lived about three miles from the Mission Hall and cycled that distance each way twice weekly in all weathers. Although a busy housewife with a husband and four sons to cater for, Sunday evening always found her in her place of worship. Her life was devoted to prayer and week by week she poured out her heart before God for the people of Craigantlet and farther afield. There was no one within easy reach of the Hall who was uncared for by her and whose name had not been mentioned in her prayers. When she died in 1980 a Memorial Service was held for her in the Mission Hall, addressed by her minister the Reverend (later Doctor) Rodney Sterritt of Greenwell Street Presbyterian Church in Newtownards. She was warmly spoken of, and many of her prayers have been answered, even after her death. Jack her youngest and only remaining son is still a participating member of the Prayer Union and has attended faithfully since his youngest days.

Mrs. Agnes McKee was another staunch supporter of the Prayer Union for many years. She gave hospitality to the Pilgrims during evangelistic campaigns, making them feel a part of her family and the work of the Faith Mission was always near and dear to her heart. Her only daughter Margaret joined the ranks of the Mission and served as a Pilgrim from 1962 until her marriage to Tom Scott in 1966, when they both left for a life of missionary service in Brazil. Although this meant long separations during which she missed out on the joys of being a grandmother, Mrs. McKee would not have had it otherwise. Despite the early loss of her husband and two eldest sons, her Christian courage and faithfulness never wavered and she remained a kindly friend and an example to us all. Her youngest son David is the present Prayer Union representative and has inherited her qualities of loyalty and steadfastness.

Miss Edith Milligan was also a staunch prayer warrior dedicated to the cause of evangelism and mission. When she learnt to drive she used her new accomplishment in the service of others and as a result Mrs. McCracken no longer had to cycle to the meetings. They travelled together happily for many years. Edith lived to a ripe old age, and in 2008 she went home to be with her Lord whom she had loved and served so well.

Children's activities in the Mission Hall were always conducted by ladies. From my very young days I remembered attending the Sunrise Band and I can still visualise the shining magazine we were given with a picture of a rising sun on its cover. This little group was led by Miss Jean Musgrave, who also played the organ for a number of years. Looking back I realise she could only have been in her teenage years but, child-like, I believed that anyone who had left school was grown up and therefore old. However she had a sweet maturity and a gentle manner and I never remember her having to scold any of us for bad behaviour. She taught us the familiar hymns and action choruses that have stood the test of time. She read us a Bible story and conducted Bible searches and games. It was under her teaching and example that I took my first faltering steps of faith. After her marriage, her sister Wilhelmina carried on these meetings for a number of years and more latterly a Child Evangelism Fellowship worker led a Good News Club which was well supported in the 70s.

Under New Management

When Mr. Hanna retired it was the end of an era. He had
been in charge for over forty years and we began to think
him irreplaceable. Happily a younger energetic Christian
man had come to live on the Ballybarnes Road. Mr. David
McGilton was originally from Newtownards but his wife
Aileen was a local girl who lived for many years at Cree's
Corner. When invited to take charge of the Sunday services
David agreed readily, and with Aileen and their daughter
Christine, threw himself wholeheartedly into the work. It is
said that a Boys' Brigade member will always be known by
his walk, and this was true of David in every sense of the
word. He was a man of great confidence who led from the
front. Having a fine baritone voice, he conducted the
singing, which improved considerably under his direction.
He drew up a list of various speakers and the services gained
a new momentum due to his enthusiasm. He was affable,
approachable and well respected, but above all a man of
sterling Christian character. They were happy days with
David McGilton at the helm, David McKee as the Prayer
Union representative and another David - David Mullan,
who acted as a one-man welcoming committee, standing in
the cold reception area giving out hymn books. David
Mullan came to live in Craigantlet in 1978 when he married
Gwen Morrison, a local girl whose mother and uncle had

been regular Mission Hall attenders. By coincidence David and Gwen's house was built on the site of Samuel Montgomery's old house. They were each in their turn 'good stewards and 'door keepers in the house of God'. The three Davids were ably assisted by Jack McCracken, who took responsibility of car parking and directing the traffic onto what had become a very busy road. Cars travelled at great speed over the brow of the hill past the Mission Hall entrance, so it became necessary for each car to be directed individually through the gates and into the stream of traffic. This became Jack's self-imposed task and was performed so thoroughly that no mishaps occurred and no complaints were received. Jack also performed a good number of manual tasks on the site. As a prominent dairy farmer, it seemed fitting that he should supply milk for the Conference, but he also provided water for the tea and washing up. Incredible as it may seem, in all the years of its existence the Tin Tabernacle had no water supply either on tap or on site. Jack's wife Alice baked the lightest and most delicious sponge cakes, which were much in demand by Conference-goers. Their kindness and generosity is well known and valued by their many friends and neighbours.

One hesitates to say that anyone dies prematurely, for all our lives are lived within the parameters of God's grace, or as a Psalmist expresses it so poetically, "All the days ordained for me were written in your book before one of them came to be" (NIV) but sadly David McGilton did not reach advanced years and went home to be with the Lord in 2000. During his brief illness he displayed great Christian fortitude and unshrinking faith. Aileen, already suffering from a debilitating illness, went with Christine to live in Scotland near her married daughter Pamela who tended her lovingly for the next few short years that she remained on earth. She kept in touch for as long as her health permitted, and enjoyed hearing news from her old neighbours. Her final letter was one of joyful anticipation and kindly thoughts to us all. During a well-spent life, she performed many acts of charity and was awarded the OBE for her services to disabled children.

Change and Decay

Time moved on into the first years of the new millennium, and it seemed that the whole of the media believed that this old world of ours was fast spinning to an end. Gospel preachers had often been derided for this Biblical prediction, but now it seemed that scientists believed we ourselves were about to press the self-destruct button and we were consistently being offered advice on how to save the planet. One thing became apparent to us all at Craigantlet - our much loved little Tin Tabernacle - was coming to the end of its useful life. The roof leaked (but only a little and only when it rained!) and destructive rust had set in around its foundation. It had withstood wind and weather for nearly ninety years and corrugated iron is not meant to last forever. To the best of my knowledge the person most responsible for its maintenance over recent years, surprisingly, was Tom Scott 'the man from Brazil'. During times of deputation and longer periods of home assignment, both he and Margaret threw themselves wholeheartedly into the service of the Mission Hall. Tom, a man of mature spiritual insight, is nothing if not practical. Seeing a job needing to be done, his first instinct is to roll up his sleeves. It was he who replaced the east facing windows and added the fine heavy door, but there was no denying that the little building was living on borrowed time. Sunday evening services were conducted only on a monthly basis, for although there were still a few dozen loyal supporters, we felt that bringing speakers to our little outpost of the empire was literally preaching to the converted. The Prayer Union still kept its weekly slot each Tuesday. By a strange coincidence the little building had never looked more attractive inside. It was curtained, carpeted and cushioned and painted in soft pastel colours. It had a quiet welcoming dignity and always felt warm and comfortable. This was due to a united effort under the direction of David and Hazel McKee who have good taste in these matters. There is much to be said for "growing old gracefully" in this way, and it is always a delight to meet old friends who, although outwardly less attractive and useful, have acquired an inner beauty of spirit, a mature wisdom and a cheerful attitude. Such attributes are often difficult to sustain, especially in the presence of pain and weakness, but surely worth cultivating if we are to enjoy our golden years to the full.

Crossroads Church

During this period a new Fellowship was beginning to flourish in our midst - Crossroads Evangelical Church. It is well known that the Orange Order welcomes Evangelical groups into its halls, and Craigantlet Orange Lodge is no exception. The doors of the Orange Hall were opened to Crossroads Church, a movement that began in Dundonald and which gradually, over the years, won over some of the young people of the district and appeared to prosper while we were in decline. When in 2000 the Mission Hall committee was approached by the Oversight of Crossroads Church with a view to taking over the Mission Hall site, its offer was received favourably. A verse from Deuteronomy Chapter 2 verse 3, "You have compassed this mountain long enough", seemed to confirm that their offer was an answer to our prayers. At a meeting between representatives of both fellowships, the site legally became the property of Crossroads Church. A final service of thanksgiving conducted by Trevor Matthews (Faith Mission) was held in the Hall on the third of November 2001 and with due regard to health and safety, the building was demolished soon afterwards. The Tin Tabernacle was no more, but its memory lingers on in the hearts of those who held it dear. It is a treasury from our past, a House of God built and lovingly furnished by our forefathers as an act of thanksgiving to God for the movement of the Holy Spirit which took place in 1911. The words of Solomon, the wisest man of the ancient world, come to mind. "But will God indeed dwell on the earth? Behold the Heavens and Heaven of Heavens cannot contain Thee, how much less this house that I have builded."

Prayer Union Members with representatives of Crossroads Church Dinner 2001
L-R (br) Margaret Scott, Hazel McKee, Margaret Colville,
Jean Graham, Nan Magowan, Jean Shields, Alice McCracken
(br) David McKee, Jack McCracken, Tommy Scott
with members of the Crossroads Church

Looking Forward

I would not have you think that this little volume is merely a sad trip down memory lane; the nostalgic story of a noble venture of faith that flourished and then withered on the vine. For Craigantlet Prayer Union lives on due, I believe, mainly to the inspiration of the present leaders David and Hazel McKee. It was they who rallied the weary little band of believers by opening up their home on the first Tuesday of each month for a renewed and growing Prayer Union. Since their return from Brazil, Tom and Margaret Scott have hosted the little gathering bi-monthly. So we meet in blissful comfort, to hear news of the Faith Mission and other missionary endeavours, and if we linger over a welcome cup of tea who can blame us? The numbers have more than doubled and it is a joy to welcome so many others who share our interests. David McKee and Margaret Scott are third generation members of the Prayer Union and so too is Miss Margaret Lindsay who plays the organ for the services. She is also a granddaughter of foundation member Samuel McKee. Continuity is surely a sign of God's covenant blessing, but does not preclude others who bring insights that broaden our horizons and provide fresh inspiration. The centenary year will be 2011 and, God willing, we hope to celebrate it joyfully whether here on earth or with those we have loved and lost awhile.

It is my great wish and prayer that this little record of events will be a means of blessing to everyone who reads it and a source of encouragement and inspiration to all who follow in the footsteps of the pioneers of Craigantlet Mission Hall - "To God be the glory great things He has done."

Founder of the Faith Mission
"The Chief"
John George Govan

Acknowledgements

The greatest blessing of my adult life has been my family. The fact that they live near me is useful for I frequently need their help; but it is happy too, for it means that I can follow the accomplishments of my sons, daughters-in-law, and grandchildren with pride and joy. It is to all of them that I dedicate this little volume.

I specially want to thank Paul for the editing and early preparation of the text for publication; Mark, who designed the cover, arranged the sequence of hymns and photographs and liaised with the publisher; Andrew, for his delightful pen and ink vignettes; and Lois, who gave up precious holiday time to type the manuscript.

I am indebted to the late Alexander Hanna for historical details, as indicated in the text. He always spoke enthusiastically about the origin of the Hall, and I was an attentive listener.

Finally, I thank the members of Craigantlet Prayer Union, past and present, for their interest, encouragement and for supplying names and dates that eluded me. I trust that this little journey into the past will evoke happy memories of bygone days and friends long loved and "lost awhile".

The path of the just is as the shining light, that shineth more and more unto the perfect day.

PUBLICATIONS

Published and Printed by Award Publishing
email: cedricwilson@live.co.uk